sleepover Girls crafts

Snap books

Amazing
OUTDOOR ART
You Can Make and Share

by Mari Bolte

illustrated by Paula Franco

CAPSTONE PRESS
a capstone imprint

Table of Contents

Pack your bags for fun with the Sleepover Girls! Every Friday, Maren, Ashley, Delaney, and Willow get together for crafts, fashion, cooking, and, of course, girl talk! Read the books, get to know the girls, and dive in to this book of cool projects that are Sleepover Girl staples!

Light a candle that reminds you of your last vacay, or dance with a flower crown you've DIYed. March boldly into the wilderness with a bottle of cooling spray and homemade insect repellent. Grab some glue, phone some friends, and start crafting with your very own Sleepover Girls.

MEET THE SLEEPOVER GIRLS!

Willow Marie Keys

Patient and kind, Willow is a wonderful confidante and friend. (Just ask her twin, Winston!) She is also a budding artist with creativity for miles. Willow's Bohemian style suits her flower child within.

Maren Melissa Taylor

Maren is what you'd call "personality-plus"—sassy, bursting with energy, and always ready with a sharp one-liner. You'll often catch Maren wearing a hoodie over a sports tee and jeans. An only child, Maren has adopted her friends as sisters.

Ashley Francesca Maggio

Ashley is the baby of a lively Italian family. This fashionista-turned-blogger is on top of every style trend via her blog, Magstar. Vivacious and mischievous, Ashley is rarely sighted without her beloved "purse puppy," Coco.

Delaney Ann Brand

Delaney's smart, motivated, and always on the go! You'll usually spot low-maintenance Delaney in a ponytail and jeans (and don't forget her special charm bracelet, with charms to symbolize her Sleepover Girl buddies.)

Flower Crown

Ashley picked a flower crown to show off Willow's Bohemian style. Make your own with just a few easy-to-find items, pair it with a pretty sundress, and you're ready for an outdoor concert.

WHAT YOU'LL NEED

grapevine floral wire
ribbon
hot glue and hot glue gun
wire cutters
green floral wire
fresh or silk flowers

1 With an adult's help, measure and cut a piece of grapevine wire long enough to wrap loosely around your head.

2 Wrap ribbon around the crown to hide the wire. Secure the ends with hot glue.

3 Once you have a design in mind, use the green floral wire to wrap flowers around the crown. Use several loops of wire to ensure the flowers are attached snugly.

4 Continue placing and wrapping flowers until the crown is to your liking.

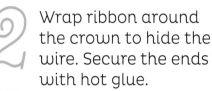

5 Wrap more ribbon around any uncovered parts of the crown.

6 Loop long lengths of ribbon around the back of the crown for a train.

Solar Jars

The sun will go down, but that doesn't mean the sleepover is over! Light up the night with these DIY solar lights.

WHAT YOU'LL NEED

decoupage glue

food coloring

small mouth mason jars, quart sized

solar garden stakes

hot glue and hot glue gun

1 Cover your work surface well with newspaper or paper towels.

2 In a small bowl, mix several tablespoons of decoupage glue with 12-15 drops of food coloring. Thin the glue with a tablespoon of water.

3 Pour the glue and water mixture into a mason jar. Spin the jar to coat the entire inside of the jar. Pour the excess glue and water back into the bowl.

4 Place a cooling rack on your work surface. Set the jar upside down on the cooling rack. Let the jar dry for half an hour.

5 Have an adult preheat an oven to 225 degrees Fahrenheit (107 degrees Celsius). Place jars upside-down on a baking sheet lined with waxed paper. Then set them in the oven and bake for 10 minutes.

6 Have the adult flip the jars over and put them back in the oven for another 30 minutes. Let jars cool.

7 Remove the stem from the garden stakes. Set the solar cap inside the jar. Use hot glue to secure in place.

Call to Nature

One of Willow's favorite places in the world is Whidbey Island. With her hand-crafted cell phone cover, she can carry a bit of the island with her everywhere she goes.

WHAT YOU'LL NEED

dried pressed flowers

plain or clear cell phone cover

craft glue

50/50 clear casting epoxy resin

glitter (optional)

craft stick

cotton swabs and rubbing alcohol

1 Protect your work surface with newspaper. Arrange the flowers on the cell phone cover until you have a design you like. Glue the flowers in place.

2 Prepare the epoxy using the directions on the package. Add glitter, if desired.

3 Slowly pour the resin onto your case. Start with a small amount. You can always add more later.

4 Use the craft stick to spread the resin toward the edges of the case. Use cotton swabs dipped in rubbing alcohol to clean any drips.

5 Continue spreading resin until the entire back of the case and all the flowers are covered.

6 Let the resin dry for one to two hours. Add another coat of resin if necessary.

TIP:
If you can't find pressed flowers in stores or online, you can make your own! Sandwich flowers between paper towels and set inside a heavy book for at least a week. For faster results, use an iron on low heat. (Do not add water.) Press the iron over the paper towels for 10 to 15 seconds. Let the paper towel cool and check on the flowers. Repeat heating and checking until the flowers are stiff and dry.

Clay Pot *Wind Chimes*

These clay pot wind chimes create a calming, soothing sound—something Maren's going to need once in a while now that she's got younger step-siblings to deal with.

WHAT YOU'LL NEED

acrylic paint
and paintbrushes

three to four small clay
pots with drainage holes

waterproof spray sealer

4 ½ feet (1.4 meters) twine

S-hook

large washers or beads

1. Paint clay pots with your desired pattern. Let dry completely.

2. Spray pots with sealant. Let the sealant dry completely. Add a second coat, if desired.

3. Tie one end of the twine to the S-hook. Thread the other end through the bottom of a pot. Tie a knot to secure the pot in place.

4. Tie a washer or bead in place so it sits inside the pot.

5. Repeat tying pots and washers evenly down the length of the twine.

6. When you run out of pots and washers, thread a few extra beads to the end of the twine. Trim excess twine, if necessary.

Cooling Spray

Hydrate naturally with a spritz of this refreshing spray. Carry it with you on walks and nature hikes to stay cool.

WHAT YOU'LL NEED

two teabags of green tea

cucumber

1 tablespoon (15 milliliters) fresh lemon juice

1 tablespoon aloe vera gel

peppermint essential oil

spray bottle

1 Prepare a double-strong batch of green tea according to package directions. Place it in the refrigerator to cool.

2 With an adult's help, peel and roughly chop the cucumber. Place the cucumber in a blender or food processor and blend until liquefied.

3 Place the cucumber in a fine sieve and press gently to separate the solids from the liquids. Discard solids.

4 Mix ¼ cup (60 mL) of tea with 2 tablespoons (30 mL) cucumber juice. Add lemon juice, aloe vera, and 2-3 drops peppermint essential oil.

5 Pour mixture into spray bottle. Store in the refrigerator for up to a week. Shake before use. Spray as needed for a cooling effect.

TIPS:
If you don't have a sieve, put the cucumber in a clean kitchen towel. Twist the towel closed and squeeze the cucumber juice out that way.

Don't toss extra tea, cucumber juice, or lemon juice! Freeze in a zip-top sandwich bag or in an ice cube tray. Defrost as needed.

Photo *Feeder*

Throw the birds an unforgettable tea party by bringing some indoor charm to the outdoors.

WHAT YOU'LL NEED

shadow box

¾-inch (2-centimeter) diameter wooden dowel

spray sealer

industrial-strength polyurethane glue

teacup and saucer

screw hook

chain

birdseed

1 In a well-ventilated area, spray the shadow box and dowel with spray sealer. Let dry completely.

2 Use polyurethane glue to attach the teacup to the saucer. Let dry completely.

3 With an adult's help, cut a 3-inch (7.6 cm) long piece from the dowel. Glue the dowel to the bottom of the saucer. Hold in place until the glue is set, and then let dry completely.

4 Center the dowel at the bottom of the shadow box and attach with glue. Let set completely, and then let dry overnight.

5 Screw the hook to the top of the shadow box.

TIPS:
Fill teacup with water, fruit, suet, or fabric scraps and sprinkle birdseed around the saucer.

Use the teacup as a planter instead of a bird feeder.

6 Attach the chain to the hook to hang. Fill teacup with birdseed.

Bug-Off Bars

Keep the flies at bay with an all-natural repellent. It's safer for you, better for the environment, and so easy to make!

WHAT YOU'LL NEED

1 cup (240 mL) coconut oil

¼ cup (60 mL) dried rosemary

1 teaspoon (5 mL) whole cloves

2 tablespoons (30 mL) dried thyme

1 cinnamon stick

¼ cup dried catnip

1 tablespoon (15 mL) dried mint

rind from one lemon

fine mesh sieve or cheesecloth

½ cup (120 mL) cocoa butter

½ cup beeswax

empty twist-up tubes or deodorant sticks

1 Place the coconut oil, herbs, spices, and lemon rind in a large mason jar with a lid, and cover.

2 Set the mason jar in a slow cooker. Fill the slow cooker about halfway with water. Set on low and leave overnight. Swirl the jar occasionally.

3 With an adult's help, strain the oil through a sieve or cheesecloth and discard the solids. Place the oil in a microwave-safe bowl and add the cocoa butter and beeswax.

4 Microwave for 30 seconds. Remove the bowl from the microwave and stir. Repeat heating and stirring until beeswax is completely melted.

5 Pour mixture into push tubes. Let sit until completely solid.

TIP:
If you can't find twist-up tubes, pour the oil mixture into lip balm tubes, soap or candy molds, muffin tins, or silicone cupcake liners.

6 To use, rub bars directly onto exposed skin.

Cove Candles

Light up your imagination with your favorite seaside vacay jarred and ready to go.

WHAT YOU'LL NEED

2 cups (480 mL) Epsom salt

blue food coloring

zinc core candle wick

glue dots

clear bowl

seashells

gel wax

1 Pour half the salt into a zip-top sandwich bag. Add 2-3 drops of food coloring. Seal the bag and shake until all the salt is colored. Repeat with more food coloring if a darker shade is desired. Once the salt is absorbed, open the bag and let the salt dry completely.

Wrap one end of the candle wick around a pencil. Rest the pencil on top of the clear bowl. Pull out enough wick to reach the bottom of the bowl. Stick a glue dot to the end of the wick and use it to hold the wick in place.

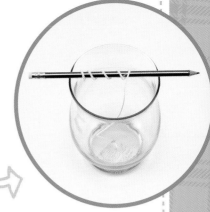

Layer salt at the bottom of the bowl, alternating blue salt with uncolored salt. Repeat until the salt layers are as thick as desired.

4 Arrange seashells on top of the salt. Press gently into the salt or use glue dots to hold the seashells in place.

Have an adult melt the wax in a double boiler over low heat. Stir often. When the wax is completely melted, slowly pour it into the glass bowl.

When the wax has cooled, trim the wick to just below the rim of the bowl.

Portable Paint

Willow paints landscapes to capture the world around her. This portable painting kit is perfect for her hikes through Whidbey Island!

WHAT YOU'LL NEED

two clean, empty gum trays

metal mint tin

tube watercolor paints

sponge

watercolor paper

small binder with plastic sleeves

hole punch

9 x 12 inch (23 x 30.5 cm) piece of felt

chalk

craft knife

watercolor brushes and pencils

ribbon

Watercolors

1 Trim gum trays to fit inside metal tin, if necessary. Fill each well of the trays with tube watercolors. Let dry completely.

2 Cut the sponge to fit inside the tin's lid. The sponge is for cleaning your brushes while painting.

Paper

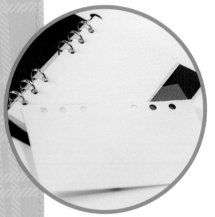

1 Punch holes in the watercolor paper so it fits in the binder. Trim the sides if necessary.

2 Place the plastic sleeve under the first piece of paper. This will both protect the rest of the paper and hold any finished art pieces.

Brush Carrier

1 Lay the piece of felt flat, with the long edge facing you. Use a ruler to divide the felt into thirds and mark with chalk.

2 Use chalk to make ½ inch (1.3 cm) wide dashes above and below the divide lines.

3 Cut the dashes with a craft knife. Slide watercolor brushes and pencils through the slits.

4 Roll the felt up with the brushes and pencils inside. Tie the brush carrier shut with a piece of ribbon.

Tabletop Water Garden

This tabletop water garden makes an awesome centerpiece on the Taylor dinner table. Add a fish and you've got the perfect pet.

WHAT YOU'LL NEED

water bottle

gravel or other small rocks

small water plant

large container, such as a pot, jar, or vase

small fish (optional)

1 Cut the bottom off the water bottle. With an adult's help, punch holes in the bottom of the bottle. Fill the bottom of the bottle with gravel.

2 Carefully transplant the plant to the water bottle. Add enough dirt to cover the roots. Pack the dirt down gently, then cover with more gravel.

3 Place the plant in a sink. Carefully pour water onto the plant until completely saturated. Let soak for at least an hour. Pour more water onto the plant. Continue watering and soaking until the water runs clear.

4 Put some gravel in the large container. Set the plant inside the container and use the gravel to hold it in place.

5 Slowly pour water into the container. Let the dirt settle and the water come to room temperature, at least overnight, before adding a fish.

TIPS:

Possible water plants include taro, water hyacinth, miniature cattails, water lettuce, and miniature water lilies. Some plants need to be submerged under a certain amount of water, or submerged completely, so keep your container depth in mind when selecting plants.

If you add a fish, do some research before buying. Some species will eat your water plants. Barbs, some tetras, and betta fish are a few options. Be sure your fish has clean water available at all times, and buy fish food if it's a carnivorous species.

Seed Bomb Pops

It's no surprise that earthy Willow loves wildflowers. She makes her own seed bombs to share blooms with all the Sleepover Girls.

WHAT YOU'LL NEED

rubber gloves

2 tablespoons (30 mL) wildflower seeds

3 tablespoons (45 mL) compost

1/3 cup (80mL) powdered clay

used coffee grounds, completely dried

used tea leaves, completely dried

lollipop sticks

washi tape

permanent marker

1 Wear gloves for cleanliness. Mix the seeds and compost together.

*

TIP:
Washi tape is biodegradable and made with natural paper and rubber adhesive. If you can't find washi tape, be sure you use another type of biodegradable tape.

2 Stir in powdered clay. Add water until the mixture is a moist dough.

3 Shape dough into balls. Roll some balls in coffee grounds. Roll others in tea leaves.

4 Remove one glove and use a clean hand to press lollipop sticks into balls. Let dry 24 to 48 hours.

5 Fold a strip of washi tape around the top of the pop to make a flag. Use permanent marker to write instructions or seed types on the flag.

TIPS:
Powdered clay can be found at art supply stores.

You can find wildflower seeds online, at garden centers and nurseries, and through seed companies. Be sure the seeds you use are native to your area. You can also use other types of seeds, such as herb or vegetable seeds.

6 To use, place seed pops in a sunny spot and water regularly. Do not bury pops; this will prevent the seeds from germinating.

Energy Bars

Whether you're spending the day hiking or the night hanging with your sleepover friends, you need to keep your energy up. These tasty energy bars will do the job!

WHAT YOU'LL NEED

FOR THE FILLING:

2 tablespoons (30 mL) cornstarch

2 cups (480 mL) strawberries, mashed

¼ cup (60 mL) honey

FOR THE BARS:

2 ¼ cup (600 mL) quick oats

1 cup (240 mL) chocolate hazelnut spread

¼ cup honey

¼ cup applesauce

1 large egg, beaten

½ teaspoon (2.5 mL) almond extract

½ cup (120 mL) almonds

½ cup white chocolate chips

1 Mix cornstarch with an equal amount of water.

2 In a small sauce pot, combine strawberries and honey. Have an adult bring the mixture to a boil, stirring often. Remove from heat and stir in cornstarch until fully combined and lump-free. Set aside to cool.

3 Preheat oven to 325 degrees Fahrenheit (163 degrees Celsius.) Line an 8-inch (20.3 cm) square baking pan with tinfoil.

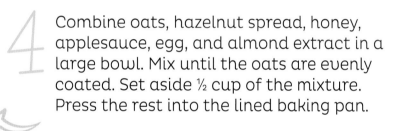

4 Combine oats, hazelnut spread, honey, applesauce, egg, and almond extract in a large bowl. Mix until the oats are evenly coated. Set aside ½ cup of the mixture. Press the rest into the lined baking pan.

5 Spread the cooled strawberry filling over the oats.

6 Add the almonds and chips to the reserved oat mixture. Mix well, then sprinkle over the top of the filling. Firmly press the sprinkled oats into the strawberries.

7 Bake for 25-30 minutes or until lightly browned. Let cool completely before cutting into bar shapes.

Outdoor *Blanket*

A comfy blanket is essential for a successful picnic, and a bright pattern is sure to make it more fun! Make your own for the perfect picnic style.

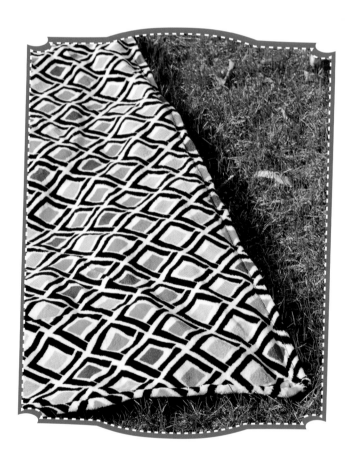

WHAT YOU'LL NEED

fleece blanket

vinyl tablecloth

sewing machine (or needle and thread)

two 12-inch (30.5 cm) pieces of ribbon

sewing pins

double fold bias tape

grommet pliers and 3/8-inch (1 cm) grommets

1 Lay the blanket flat on your work surface. Set the tablecloth over the blanket. The decorative sides of both the blanket and the tablecloth should be facing out.

SEWING TIPS:

This craft will go much faster with a sewing machine. If you don't have a sewing machine, follow these simple sewing instructions.

Slide the thread through the eye of the needle. Tie the end of the thread into a knot. Poke the needle through the underside of the fabric. Pull the thread through the fabric to the knotted end. Poke your needle back through the fabric and up again to make a stitch.

Continue weaving the needle in and out of the fabric, making small stitches in a straight line. When you are finished sewing, make a loose stitch. Thread the needle through the loop and pull tight. Cut off remaining thread.

2 Trim the tablecloth to the same size as the blanket.

3 Sew the fleece to the tablecloth.

4 Sew the ribbon near one of the corners of the blanket. The ribbon strings will be used to tie the blanket together when it's rolled up.

5 Open the bias tape and pin it along the edge of the blanket. Then sew in place.

6 Follow package instructions to punch a grommet into each corner of the blanket.

7 To use, set blanket vinyl-side-down on the ground. Use golf tees or camping stakes through the grommet holes to keep blanket flat.

Read More

Green, Gail. *Paper Artist: Creations Kids Can Fold, Tear, Wear, or Share.* Paper Creations. North Mankato, Minn.: Capstone, 2013.

Grimshaw, Melanie. *Make It!* Art Smart. Mankato, Minn.: QEB Publishing, 2012.

Petelinsek, Kathleen. *Crafting With Tissue Paper.* How-To Library. Ann Arbor, Mich.: Cherry Lake Publishing, 2014.

Snap Books are published by Capstone, 1710 Roe Crest Drive, North Mankato, Minnesota 56003.

www.capstonepub.com

Library of Congress Cataloging-in-Publication Data
Bolte, Mari.
  Amazing outdoor art you can make and share /
By Mari Bolte.
    pages cm.—(Snap books. Sleepover girls crafts)
  Summary: "Step-by-step instructions, tips, and full-color photographs will help teens and tweens create outdoor-themed projects"—Provided by publisher.
  ISBN 978-1-4765-0229-8 (library binding)
  ISBN 978-1-4914-6543-1 (paperback)
1. Nature craft—Juvenile literature. 2. Handicraft for girls—Juvenile literature. I. Title.

TT157.B68 2016
745.5—dc23   2015023314

Designer: Tracy Davies McCabe
Craft Project Creators:
The Occasions Group
Creative Director: Nathan Gassman
Production Specialist: Laura Manthe

Photo Credits:
All photos by The Occasions Group Photo Studio

Artistic Effects:
Shutterstock

Printed in the United States of America in North Mankato, Minnesota.
032015   008823CGF15